Celebrating your year

1950

a very special year for

Let's flashback to 1950, a very special year.

Was this the year you were born?

Was this the year you were married?

Whatever the reason, this book is a celebration of your year,

THE YEAR 1950.

Turn the pages to discover a book packed with fun-filled fabulous facts. We look at the people, the places, the politics and the pleasures that made 1950 unique and helped shape the world we know today.

So get your time-travel suit on, and enjoy this trip down memory lane, to rediscover what life was like, back in the year 1950.

First flight or fiftieth, you'll be glad you chose TWA

Don't look for just *one* reason why more than a million passengers a year fly TWA. For it's not *routes* alone, or *speed* alone, or *service* alone, or *dependability* alone that leads to such loyalty. It's the happy combination of all these factors that makes one airline stand out.

TWA is the only U.S. airline connecting 56 U.S. cities with key points in Europe, Africa and Asia. TWA's speed is unsurpassed. TWA's magnificent Constellations are world-proved for both dependability and comfort.

But the real "plus" is TWA's PEOPLE. Million-mile Flight Captains, courteous, capable hostesses, skilled maintenance helpers all are part of TWA's smoothly functioning team of thousands working together to make your trip fast, comfortable, safe.

Did you know that TWA hostesses are specially trained and equipped to help mothers care for babies... with diapers, bottles, and a kit of supplies?

Contents

1950 American Family Life

Imagine if time-travel was a reality, and one fine morning you wake up to find yourself flashed back in time, back to the year 1950.

What would life be like for a typical family, in a typical town, somewhere in America?

A family cooling off outside their home in the 1950s.

The post-war boom gave us booming birth numbers, booming suburbs, a booming economy, and the booming trappings of the consumerist culture we still enjoy today. With the stringent post-war years well behind us, the rising middle classes were feeling an urgent need to spend.

An unprecedented 3.6 million babies were born in 1950 (up from 2.8 million at the end of the war five years earlier).[1] And to house this increased demand, we built almost 1.5 million new houses, most of them in the new suburban developments springing up on the outskirts of towns.

The median income was $3,300[1] a year, unemployment was 4.3% and falling, with GDP at 8.7%.[2]

Average costs in 1950 [3]	
New house	$8,450
New car	$1,150
Television	$250
Clock Radio	$60
A gallon of gas	$0.18

Artist's impression of a family outing in 1950 America.

The family was everything. Fathers commuted to earn a salary. Wives were encouraged to quit their jobs and stay at home. Children walked to school and played outdoors in their well manicured gardens.

Families dined together, watched television together, and enjoyed leisure time and outings together.

[1] census.gov/library/publications.html.
[2] thebalance.com/unemployment-rate-by-year-3305506 and thebalance.com/us-gdp-by-year-3305543.
[3] thepeoplehistory.com/1950.html.

Joining the television in our families' list of must-haves were: defrost refrigerators, fully-automatic washing machines, front-loading dryers, vacuum cleaners, air-conditioning and heating units, milkshake makers, and a multitude of other kitchen gadgets and home appliances. In addition we needed a family car or two, bicycles, motorcycles, hiking, camping, picnic gear and much, much more.

An energetic and persuasive advertising industry, through TV, radio and print, ensured we always knew what our next purchase needed to be.

"At Last! I'm Free . . .

thanks to my new

WESTINGHOUSE **FROST-FREE*** REFRIGERATOR"

An safety educational magazine from 1950.

But beneath the appearance of abundance and domestic bliss, Americans were deeply concerned. The Soviets had detonated an atomic bomb in 1949, setting in motion a nuclear race between the two superpowers—the Cold War.

By 1950 both powers were striving to build an even more powerful weapon—the hydrogen bomb.

We would endure another 40 years of tension between the two super-powers before the Cold War finally ended with the dissolution of the Soviet Union in 1991.

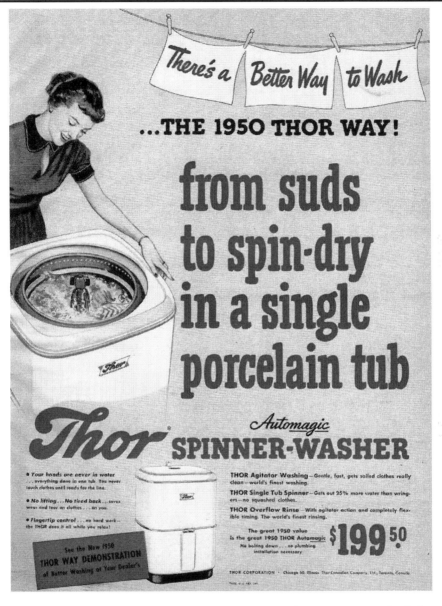

Your hands are never in water... everything done in one tub. You never touch clothes until ready for the line.

No lifting... No tired back... saves wear and tear on clothes... on you.

Fingertip control... no hard work–the THOR does it all while you relax!

THOR Agitator Washing–Gentle, fast, gets soiled clothes really clean–world's finest washing.

THOR Single Tub Spinner–Gets out 25% more water than wringers–no squashed clothes.

THOR Overflow Rinse–With agitator action and completely flexible timing. The world's finest rinsing.

The great 1950 value is the great 1950 THOR Automagic. $199.50

No bolting down... no plumbing installation necessary.

See the New 1950 THOR WAY DEMONSTRATION of Better Washing at your Dealer's.

Austerity in the United Kingdom

Now just imagine you flashed back to a town in 1950 United Kingdom or Western Europe.

Unlike boom-time America, a very different, more restrained lifestyle would await you.

London, like many other European cities, bore the brunt of destruction from the WWII bombings. The rebuilding process was slow, hampered by a general shortage of manpower and construction materials.

In the cities there was a desperate shortage of housing to accommodate the growing population. Nearly half of those living in cities housed in private, rented, often substandard apartments. While in the country, homes often lacked water, sanitation, electricity and phones.

A London street scene in 1950.

Stifling and miserable austerity measures had been in place for the preceding ten years. On the 26th May 1950, the UK finally ended petrol rationing. However rationing of meat and other basic foods would stay in place for another four years.

The post-war baby boom, along with a shortage of funds and building materials for new schools, often resulted in crowded classes of up to 50 students in urban areas.

Children at school in England in 1950.

Elections held in February 1950 saw an unprecedented 84% voter turnout, returning the Labour Party to power with the help of the powerful trade unions.

Across the United Kingdom, taxes were high with around 6.6% of GDP spent on defence.

Average salaries were around £100.[1]

[1] historytoday.com/archive/britain-1950.

"It shines on dress parade... It proves its mettle in action!"

"It's got 'let's go' starts and 'cat's paw' stops!"

Before you buy any car, your Ford Dealer invites you to "Test Drive" the '50 Ford! "Test Drive" it for power... for comfort... for ease of handling. As for economy–the rapidly growing family of '50 Ford owners has found that this car is designed for top value in original purchase price, and top economy of operation and maintenance. And for looks– well Ford has won the Fashion Academy's Gold Medal again for 1950! See it–"Test Drive" it at your Ford Dealer's today!

"It takes the medal for Beauty and it's built to live outdoors!"

There's a Ford in your future, with a future built in!

Our Love Affair with Automobiles

In just five years since war's end, the US car industry had shifted from fabricating utilitarian war tanks and trucks, to producing fashionable consumer vehicles, the kind of which we just had to have.

There were now 40 million registered cars on US roads, up from 25 million five years earlier.[1] Our love affair with cars had begun.

Cars on a Philadelphia traffic circle, 1950.

Detroit had long been the car manufacturing hub of the country, and America led the world in car production, turning out 8 million vehicles in 1950 alone. This equated to more than 80% of all new vehicles worldwide. [1]

With a population of 1.85 million people, Detroit had become the 4th largest city in the USA.[2] And by the end of the decade, a whopping one in six adults nation-wide would be employed in the car industry.

[1] fhwa.dot.gov/ohim/summary95/mv200.pdf.
[2] theweek.com/articles/461968/rise-fall-detroit-timeline.

Our love affair with cars grew hand-in-hand with the post-war baby boom and housing construction boom. Where would we be without our cars? How else could we get from our far-flung suburban homes to our inner city offices?

The Studebaker Champion is one of the 4 lowest price largest selling cars in America!

$1487.50

Studebaker
Champion
Custom 6-pass.
2-door sedan
as shown

the "Better than ever"

Rising incomes saw car ownership soar in the year 1950. An additional 2.4 million vehicles were put on the US roads as families fled the cities for the quiet life of the suburbs.

MERCURY sport sedan—These smooth, slick lines make the six-passenger 1950 Mercury Sport Sedan a car to be admired at first sight. And your first drive will make you admire its down-to-earth roadability. Long, broad, sturdy... the "better than ever" 1950 Mercury Sport Sedan is sure to be a hit with style-wise people wherever it's seen.

Cars were no longer just a necessity; they had become an expression of our personality. Sturdy, sporty, or luxurious, cars now came in a wide range of styles, colors, and price points, with chrome, wings, stripes and fins for added personality.

Now on display... the most dramatically new car of the year! Deliberately and excitingly re-styled as no other car! Its beauty outside and inside is new, new, new!... The modern classic! See it... drive it... and compare it! And you'll learn the important difference in Chrysler's kind of beauty. For here—as nowhere else—is beauty that truly reflects the sound engineering and solid comfort and safety inside. The extra headroom, legroom, shoulder-room! The chair-height seats! The full vision all around! All the qualities that have meant so much to you have been retained! Go see your Chrysler dealer today. There's no other car like the all-new Chrysler for 1950!

the Wilshire — with 16" Picture Tube $499⁹⁵

**WITH "TRIPLE-PLAY" PHONOGRAPH! FM-AM DYNAMAGIC RADIO!
SUPER-POWERED TV CHASSIS! BUILT-IN ROTO-SCOPE ANTENNA!**

Now!... *complete home entertainment* in a magnificent hand-rubbed 18th
Century walnut console by one of the world's leading stylists. Engineered
to outperform any set, anywhere, any time! Enjoy TV pictures clear as the
movies on a huge 16" tube (almost 150 square inches) . . . so clear you can
sit as near to the screen as you please. Easy to tune as a radio. Built-in
Roto-Scope antenna assures most powerful station pick-up of all . . .
because *it's directional!* Versatile "Triple-Play" phonograph plays all records
(33⅓, 45, 78 rpm), all sizes, all automatically with one tone arm, one needle,
one spindle. Static-free Dynamagic FM-AM radio . . . ultra-compact! Generous record storage space. See your nearby Admiral dealer now!

Prices subject to change. Mahogany or blonde cabinet slightly higher. Tax extra.

ON TV!
"Stop the Music"—ABC-TV Network, Thurs.
"Lights Out"—NBC-TV Stations, Mondays

With "triple-play" phonograph! FM-AM dynamagic radio! Super-powered TV chassis! Built-in roto-scope antenna!

Now!... *Complete home entertainment* in a magnificent hand-rubbed 18th Century walnut console by one of the world's leading stylists. Engineered to outperform any set, anywhere, any time! Enjoy TV pictures clear as the movies on a huge 16" tube (almost 150 square inches)... so clear you can sit as near to the screen as you please. Easy to tune as a radio. Built-in Roto-Scope antenna assures most powerful station pick-up of all... because *it's directional!* Versatile "Triple-Play" phonograph plays all records ($33^1/_2$, 45, 78 rpm), all sizes, all automatically with one tone arm, one needle, one spindle. Static-free Dynamagic FM-AM radio... ultra-compact! Generous record storage space. See your nearby Admiral dealer now!

The Golden Age of Television

By 1950, an estimated 3.8 million American households, equivalent to 9% of the population, owned a television set.[1] And that number would increase exponentially throughout the decade as television became our number one preferred choice of entertainment.

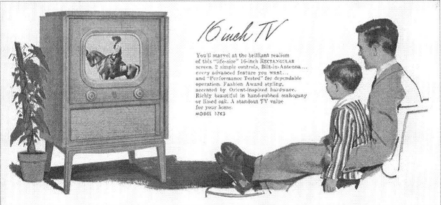

Family focussed Motorola television advertisements from 1950.

For the rising middle classes, television was much more convenient than going to a downtown cinema. It provided an increasing array of programs to watch, it was available every day of the week, and it was free to watch once purchased.

[1] americancentury.omeka.wlu.edu/items/show/136.

Most Popular Television Shows of 1950

1	Texaco Star Theater	11	Robert Montgomery Presents
2	Fireside Theater	12	Martin Kane, Private Eye
3	Philco TV Playhouse	13	Man Against Crime
4	Your Show of Shows	14	Kraft Television Theatre
5	The Colgate Comedy Hour	15	The Toast of the Town
6	Gillette Cavalcade of Sports	16	The Aldrich Family
7	The Lone Ranger	17	You Bet Your Life
8	Arthur Godfrey's Talent Scouts	18	Arthur Godfrey and His Friends
9	Hopalong Cassidy	19	Armstrong Circle Theatre
10	Mama	=	Lights Out
		=	Big Town

* From the Nielsen Media Research 1950-51 season of top-rated primetime television series.

In the early 50s, television continued to rely on live broadcasts of popular radio programs. These broadcasts were much cheaper and faster to produce than made-for-TV dramas.

Comedy-Varieties remained our most popular form of family-time TV entertainment, accounting for six of the top eight programs for the year.

Ed Sullivan, host of *The Toast of the Town* (CBS. 1948-1965).

Also keeping us glued to our screens were highly rated drama series such as *The Lone Ranger, Fireside Theater, Hopalong Cassidy,* and *Martin Kane, Private Eye.*

Clayton Moore and Jay Silverheels in *The Lone Ranger* (ABC. 1949-1957).

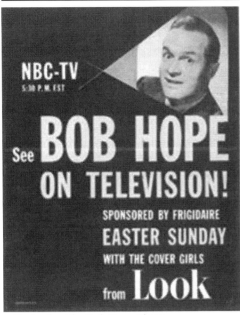

Poster for *The Bob Hope Show*
(NBC. 1950-1996, various specials).

Ralph Byrd in *Dick Tracy* (ABC. 1950-1951).

The television networks were quick to turn out new programs to keep us tuning in. Here are just a few of the new programs that aired for the first time in 1950: *The Bob Hope Show, Dick Tracy, What's My Line, The Jack Benny Program* and *You Bet Your Life* (host Groucho Marx).

George Fenneman and Groucho Marx in
You Bet Your Life (NBC-TV. 1950-1961).

The Jack Benny Program (CBS. 1950-1965).

Charles Monroe Schulz sketching Charlie Brown in 1956.

Charlie Brown in his first comic strip, 1950.

Charles M. Schultz introduced us to his Peanuts Gang on 2nd October 1950, when seven American newspapers printed his daily comic strip. Schultz was 27 years old at the time. He would go on to create another 50 years of adventures for Charlie Brown and the Gang before his retirement in 1999.

1950s   1960s   1970s   1980s   1990s

Five decades of Charlie Brown.

A 1950's comic strip showing the early version of Charlie Brown. The black t-shirt zigzag was introduced later that year.

Snoopy first appeared in a Peanuts comic strip in October 1950.

By the time of Schultz's passing in 2000, the Peanuts comic strip was syndicated in over 2,600 newspapers worldwide. The Peanuts Gang continues to inspire and enthral readers to this day, having spawned books, television shows and movies in over 25 languages.[1]

Charlie Brown, Snoopy, Linus, Lucy, Peppermint Patty, and their friends live on in the child within all of us.

[1] Details and figures from Schulzmuseum.org.

Best Ride Money Can Buy—Costs a Lot Less Money—When you go Greyhound!

Best Ride? There's a bold claim—but we sincerely believe that Greyhound gives you more relaxation (in body-contoured easy chairs), more real comfort (aboard warm, well-ventilated Super Coaches), more mental ease (behind highly-skilled drivers), and greater scenic enjoyment (along America's magnificent highways) than any other transportation in the Land!

Costs Less? The easiest way to convince yourself is by calling the nearest Greyhound station—and comparing the fares with those of any other travel. See how you save up to a third or half of every dollar—often more—by Greyhound! Compare with private car operation, and discover this: Greyhound saves you as much as 66 cents out of each dollar bill!

On 8th February 1950, Diners' Club became the first credit card to be used when its founder, Frank McNamara, paid for his dinner using a cardboard charge card and his signature.

Diners' club launched with 200 of the founder's friends as members, and 27 participating restaurants. It was marketed as an independent payment card for diners and travelers, allowing patrons to settle their bill at the end of each month through their credit account. Diners would pay $5 per year for the privilege, whilst participating establishments would be charged 7%.

By the end of the year Diners' Club would boast 20,000 members, reaching one billion by the time of its listing on the New York Stock Exchange in 1959.

An original Diners Club card from 1950.

Diners' Club also boasts the privilege of being the first charge card in Russia (1969) and in China (1980).

Frank McNamara sold his share of Diners' Club to his partners in 1952 for $200,000.

Typing all day is easy and effortless when you have an IBM Electric. All you do is "touch" the keys—the typewriter does the work. At five o'clock you'll still feel fresh and free from fatigue.

You'll like all the energy-saving features of the IBM Electric, its simple operation, its perfect impressions, its modern styling. You'll like having the world's finest typewriter for your own.

INTERNATIONAL BUSINESS MACHINES CORPORATION

IBM, Dept. A2
590 Madison Avenue, New York 22, N. Y.

☐ I'd like to see a demonstration of the IBM Electric Typewriter.

☐ Please send brochure.

Name _____

Company _____

Address _____

Typing all day is easy and effortless when you have an IBM Electric. All you do is "touch" the keys–the typewriter does the work. At five o'clock you'll still feel fresh and free from fatigue.

You'll like all the energy-saving features of the IBM Electric, its simple operation, its perfect impressions, its modern styling. You'll like having the world's finest typewriter for your own.

Following numerous clashes along the border between North and South Korea, the North Korean military forces (KPA) advanced into South Korea on 25th June 1950, marking the start of the three-year-long Korean War.

The northern socialist state, financially supported by China and the Soviet Union, sought to reunify the two Koreas under communist rule.

Newspaper headlines from the 26th June 1950.

Fearing a communist global expansion, a United Nations combined force from twenty-one countries pledged to assist the ill prepared South Korean Army. Almost 90% of the military ground personnel sent during the next three years would come from the United States.

The initial months of war saw heavy Allied losses and multiple defeats to the stronger and better equipped KPA ground troops. However, by September, the Allied and South Korean forces broke through into North Korea, pushing the KPA troops towards the border with China.

Crew of an M24 tank along the Naktong River front, 24th Aug 1950.

Grief stricken infantryman whose buddy was killed in action, Haktong-ni area, 28th Aug 1950.

Chinese tanks on parade, Beijing 1950.

On 19th October 1950, in a surprise counterattack, the Chinese Peoples Volunteer Army sent armed forces to battle alongside the KPA.

In response, the USA increased its military involvement, sending more troops to the battle front.

The Korean war ended in July 1953 with the creation of the Korean Demilitarized Zone separating the North and South Koreas. To date no peace treaty has been signed, leaving the two Koreas technically still at war.

3rd Battalion of the Royal Australian Regiment, in Korea.

Canadian Special Forces in Korea, 13th October 1950.

British units en-route to Korea, 25th August 1950.

Spy Hunt by Universal Pictures.

Guilty of Treason by Freedom Productions.

I Married a Communist by RKO Pictures.

Destination Moon by George Pal Productions.

Soviet military propaganda poster, 1950.

Bulgarian Sino-Soviet propaganda poster, 1950.

Sino-Soviet friendship
propaganda poster, 1950.

Russian Sino-Soviet propaganda poster, 1950.

South African Apartheid Laws 27th April 1950

On 27th April 1950, the white minority government of South Africa passed into law the *Group Areas Act*, formally segregating the different races based on skin color. Ownership and occupation of land would be restricted to specific racial groups within specific areas. The law strengthened the existing Apartheid policies, allowing for forcible, and often violent, removal of non-whites from white designated areas.

Protest marches and police action in South Africa, 1950.

Around the same time, several other supporting Acts of Parliament were created, each designed to cement in place the Apartheid system. These included *the Population Registration Act* of 1950, (to classify every South African according to race) and *the Immorality Act* of 1950, (to prohibit interracial marriage or sex). *The Suppression of Communism Act* of 1950 was a broadly defined act which included any opposition to government, further allowing for the suppression of the black majority.

The Acts were strengthened and amended multiple times over subsequent years.

Following decades of international condemnation and sanctions, the laws were finally repealed in 1991 with the dismantling of the Apartheid system.

Area warning signs were commonplace.

Vintage Airline Posters from 1950.

India—A Country is Born

On 26th January 1950, a new constitution was signed giving birth to the Republic of India. The new democratic country was to be organized as a federal union of territories and states, ruled under a parliamentary system.

Commemorative stamp, India 1950.

Dr. Rajendra Prasad, India's first president, at the Republic Day celebration on 26th January 1950.

The transition away from British rule was by no means a peaceful one. During the bloody partition years that followed, it is estimated that more than one million people died and 10 million were forced to relocate. The separation of the Muslim north from India resulted in the creation of the Dominion of Pakistan.

The snowman never melts in snapshots

Around home, so much happens that you don't want to forget. Fun in the snow. A new puppy or kitten. They all come back "like yesterday" when you take pictures.

With your camera ready, and two or three extra rolls of Kodak Film on hand, it's so easy to keep your snapshot record up to date. And you can give your family and friends a great treat—"the latest news"—with extra prints... Remember, the snapshots you'll want tomorrow, you must take today.

Eastman Kodak Company, Rochester 4, N. Y.

Only Eastman makes Kodak Cameras and Kodak Film

Kodak Duallex Camera makes wonderful snapshots—easily. Negative, $2^1/_4$ x $2^1/_4$. With Kodak Lens, $12.75, with Kodak f/8 Lens, $19.85. Flasholder, $3.33. Prices include Federal Tax.

The idea of a sporting competition among member countries of the British Empire was first proposed in the 19th Century and came to fruition with the 1st British Empire Games held in 1930. The 2nd and 3rd Games were held in 1934 and 1938 respectively.

Advertisement commemorating the 1950 Games.

Interrupted by the Second World War, twelve years would pass before the 4th British Empire Games could be held in Christchurch, New Zealand. Twelve Commonwealth countries sent 590 athletes to complete, with an estimated 250,000 people attending.

Now known as the Commonwealth Games, 71 nations representing one-third of the global population come together every four years,

"in the spirit of true sportsmanship ... and ... for the honour of our Commonwealth and for the glory of sport".[1]

---

[1] Oath of the Commonwealth Games.

The candy bar that's like a chocolate nut sundae!

Chocolate. First bite, chocolate... pure Mars milk chocolate, poured on thick as it'll stay!

Almonds. Then crispy, whole almonds, the expensive kind, toasted till they're gold. Plenty of them!

Nougat. Rich, creamy nougat that comes from fresh egg whites and pure sugar whipped till it's fluffy!

The boys at Mars say: "You ought to see how we put this together!"

We stir it up in the sunniest kitchens you ever saw. Sweet milk chocolate, sugar white as snow, selected meaty almonds. With strictly fresh eggs and pure, Grade A milk straight from "down on the farm"!

The Great Brink's Robbery

On 17th January 1950, a gang of eleven armed robbers pulled off a heist that was to become the "crime of the century". $1.2 million in cash and $1.6 million in checks and securities were stolen from the Brinks Building in Boston, MA.

Joseph McGinnis, 1956.

Masterminded by Joseph "Big Joe" McGinnis, the attack had been skillfully planned for more than a year. The gang had trained, rehearsed, and fabricated costumes. They also created exact copies of keys, lock cylinders and building plans. They were well prepared. Police found very little evidence at the crime scene and spent the next six years chasing dead-end leads.

On 6th January 1956, one of the gang, caught on another misdemeanor, confessed to the crime. All 11 men were arrested in the following weeks, just days before the statute of limitations was up.

The eleven Brinks robbers, 1956.

Born 3rd April 1924, Marlon Brando ranks as one of the greatest actors of all time. Following a brief six years on Broadway, he made his film debut in Fred Zimmermann's haunting drama *The Men* in 1950, and quickly become one of cinema's most sought after and highly paid actors.

Marlon Brando in *The Men* (United Artists, 1950).

A Streetcar Named Desire poster (Warner Bros. 1951).

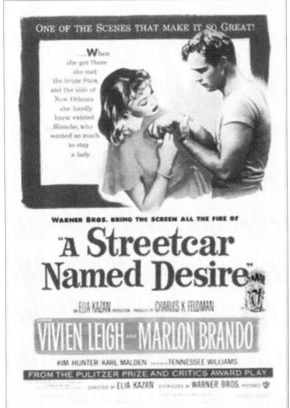

In 1951, Brando received his first Oscar nomination for his performance in *A Streetcar Named Desire*. He would go on to win two Oscars, four Golden Globes and three BAFTAs, among countless other nominations and acting awards.

In 1962 he became the first male actor to earn more than $1 million for a single film, when he was signed for *Mutiny on the Bounty*.

With his brooding good looks, sex symbol status, and a career spanning 60 years, Brando is most noted for his performances in:

Julius Caesar (1953),
On the Waterfront (1954),
The Wild One (1957),
The Godfather (1972),
Last Tango in Paris (1972)
and *Apocalypse Now* (1979).

As Marc Anthony in *Julius Caesar* (MGM. 1953).

With Mary Murphy in *The Wild One* (Colombia Pictures, 1953).

With Eva Marie Saint in *On the Waterfront* (Colombia Pictures, 1954).

As Vito Corleone in *The Godfather* (Paramount Pictures, 1972).

1950 in Cinema and Film

Bob Hope with Lucille Ball in *Fancy Pants* (Paramount Pictures, 1950).

Highest Paid Stars

1   John Wayne
2   Bob Hope
3   Bing Crosby
4   Betty Grable
5   James Stewart

Cinema attendance reached its peak in the mid 1940's and faced a steady decline throughout the 1950s. With more and more families filling their leisure time with the convenience of television, the motion-picture industry needed to find new ways to win over new audiences.

Younger audiences now had cash to spare. Movies themes adjusted to accommodate the new trends in popular culture, and to exploit the sex appeal status of young, rising stars such as Marilyn Monroe, James Dean and Marlon Brando.

Marilyn Monroe in 1953.

John Wayne in *Rio Grande* (Republic Pictures, 1950).

1950 film debuts

Marlon Brando	The Men
Tippi Hedren	The Petty Girl
Sophia Loren	Totò Tarzan
Rita Moreno	So Young, So Bad
Peter Sellers	The Black Rose
Jack Palance	Panic in the Streets
Robert Wagner	The Happy Years

* From en.wikipedia.org/wiki/1950_in_film.

Top Grossing Films of the Year

1	King Solomon's Mines	MGM	$9,955,000
2	All About Eve	20th Century Fox	$8,400,000
3	Cinderella	Disney	$8,000,000
4	Annie Get Your Gun	MGM	$7,756,000
5	Father of the Bride	MGM	$6,084,000
6	Sunset Boulevard	Paramount	$5,000,000
7	Born Yesterday	Columbia	$4,150,000
8	Wabash Avenue	20th Century Fox	$4,054,000
9	At War with the Army	Paramount	$3,100,000
10	My Blue Heaven	20th Century Fox	$3,000,000

* From en.wikipedia.org/wiki/1950_in_film by box office gross in the USA.

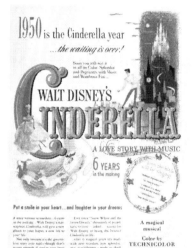

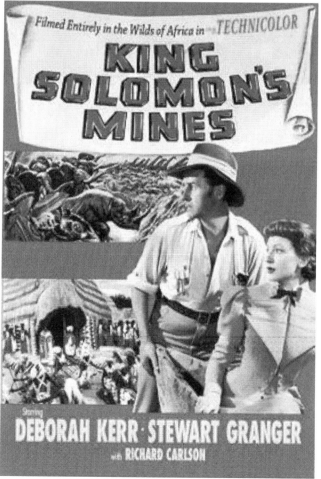

Guys and Dolls Hits Broadway

Broadway classic *Guys and Dolls* premiered on 24th November 1950, at the 46th Street Theater in New York City. It was an instant smash hit. New York critics celebrated this "perfect musical comedy", which went on for a 1200-performance run.

The musical won five Tony awards in 1951. It opened in London in 1953 and has since seen several Broadway and international revivals.

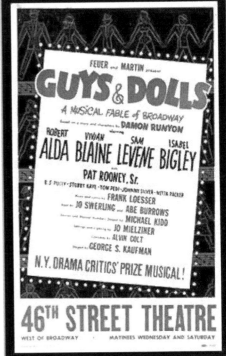

Theatrical poster from 1950.

Robert Alda and Isabel Bigley on the set of *Guys and Dolls*.

Guys and Dolls film poster (MGM. 1955).

The 1955 movie version starred Marlon Brando and Frank Sinatra, two of Hollywood's biggest names, in the leading male roles.

The Lion, the Witch and the Wardrobe 16ᵗʰ Oct 1950

Between 1950 and 1956, children's author C. S. Lewis published *The Chronicles of Narnia*, a series of seven fantasy novels set in the mythical land of Narnia. *The Lion, the Witch and the Wardrobe* was the first of the series and the best known of the seven books. The book was instantly popular with young readers.

Released on 16th October 1950, publisher Geffrey Bles feared the book would not sell well. At the time children's books were realistic in nature. Fantasy books were considered inappropriate and potentially harmful to children.

The book has since been published in nearly 50 languages, remaining popular till this day. It has been adapted for theater, television and film. Since 2005, Disney has released the films of the first three books in the series: *The Lion, the Witch and the Wardrobe, Prince Caspian* and *The Voyage of the Dawn Treader*.

1950 Billboard Top 30 Songs

	Artist	Song Title
1	Gordon Jenkins and The Weavers	Goodnight Irene
2	Nat King Cole	Mona Lisa
3	Anton Karas	Third Man Theme
4	Gary and Bing Crosby	Sam's Song
5	Gary and Bing Crosby	Simple Melody
6	Teresa Brewer	Music, Music, Music
7	Guy Lombardo	Third Man Theme
8	Red Foley	Chattanoogie Shoe Shine Boy
9	Sammy Kaye	Harbor Lights
10	Sammy Kaye and Don Cornell	It Isn't Fair

Guy Lombardo

Nat King Cole

Sammy Kaye

Patti Page

	Artist	Song Title
11	Eileen Barton	If I Knew You Were Coming I'd have Baked A Cake
12	Kay Starr	Bonaparte's Retreat
13	Gordon Jenkins and The Weavers	Tzena, Tzena, Tzena
14	Tony Martin	There's No Tomorrow
15	Phil Harris	The Thing
16	Ames Brothers	Sentimental Me
17	Andrews Sisters and Gordon Jenkins	I Wanna Be Loved
18	Patti Page	Tennessee Waltz
19	Andrews Sisters and Gordon Jenkins	I Can Dream, Can't I
20	Tennessee Ernie Ford and Kay Starr	I'll Never Be Free

Perry Como

Bing Crosby

21	Patti Page	All My Love
22	Gordon Jenkins	My Foolish Heart
23	Ames Brothers	Rag Mop
24	Bill Snyder	Bewitched
25	Perry Como	Hoop-Dee-Doo
26	Gordon Jenkins	Bewitched
27	Ames Brothers	Can Anyone Explain?
28	Billy Eckstine	My Foolish Heart
29	Bing Crosby	Dear Hearts & Gentle Peo
30	Frankie Laine	Cry Of The Wild Goose

* From the *Billboard* top 30 singles of 1950.

Why accept less when you can be sure of complete comfort with Jockey Underwear! It fits snug as your skin, moves as you move, gives you positive masculine support. Look for the mark, "Y-FRONT," on the garment–it's your assurance that you're getting the famous Coopers product... and one of may reasons why Jockey gives you a real lift. See your dealer soon–be "Hip-Taped" for perfect fit–then feel like a million in Jockey brand Underwear! Jockey Contoured Shirts to match.

Wear Jockey Underwear made only by Coopers.
Comfort for your every need–for every occasion.

Jockey Shorts for active sport. Jockey Midway for everyday wear. Jockey Over-Knee for upper-leg protection. Jockey Longs for full-leg protection. Jockey Beilin for dress-up wear.

The famous brand of knit support underwear. Also Jockey brand Underwear in Children's sizes.

British Grand Prix at Silverstone 1950, Alfa Romeo's Giuseppe Farina leads teammate Luigi Fagioli.

The FIA[1] Formula One (F1) World Championship of Drivers inaugural season commenced in Silverstone, UK, on 13th May 1950. Six Grand Prix races held over four months in Europe, plus the Indianapolis 500, saw fourteen teams participate, along with some privately entered cars. Alfa Romeo dominated throughout with their pre-war supercharged 158. Italian Giuseppe "Nino" Farina won the championship.

[1] Fédération Internationale de l'Automobile.

1950 Poster, Monaco Grand Prix.

Giuseppe "Nino" Farina. Alfa Romeo 158.

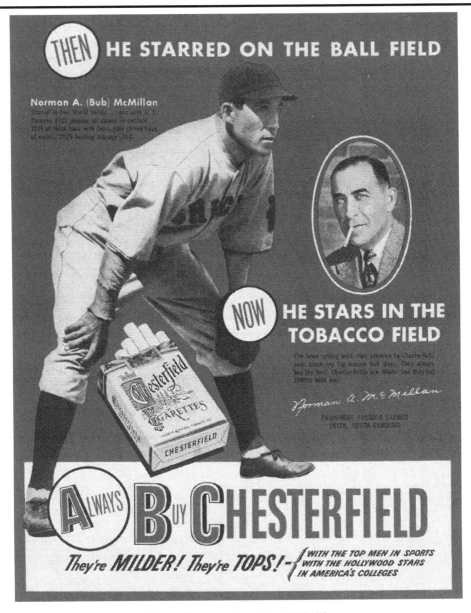

Then—He starred on the ball field.

Norman A. (Bub) McMillan—Starred in two World Series... one with N.Y. Yankees 1922 playing all games in outfield... 1929 at third base with Cubs, only stolen base of series. 1929 batting average 360.

Now—He stars in the tobacco field.

I've been selling mild, ripe tobacco to Chesterfield ever since my big-league ball days. They always buy the best. Chesterfields are Milder and they bat 1000% with me! —Norman A. McMillan. Prominent tobacco farmer, Latta, South Carolina.

Always Buy Chesterfield. They're milder! They're tops!—With the top men in sports. With the Hollywood stars. In America's colleges.

Other Sporting Events from 1950

30th Jan– Louise Brough beat Doris Hart 6-4, 3-6, 6-4 in an all-American final at the Australian Championships Women's Tennis.

14th Jan– Moroney scored cricket twin centuries for Australia in Johannesburg, South Africa.

25th Mar– Wales outclassed France, 21-0 at Cardiff to clinch the Five Nations Rugby Championship, Grand Slam and Triple Crown.

9th Apr– Jimmy Demaret became the first 3-time Masters champion at the 14th US Masters Tournament, Augusta National GC.

25th Apr– Chuck Cooper became the first African American to be drafted into the NBA (for Boston Celtics).

21st Jun– 2,000th hit for Joe DiMaggio, Yanks beat Indians 8-2.

29th Jun– US beat England 1-0 in a world cup soccer game (next win would not be until 1994).

16th Jul– FIFA World Cup Final, Estádio do Maracanã, Rio de Janeiro: Alcides Ghiggia scored a 79th minute winner as Uruguay beats Brazil, 2-1.

22nd Aug– Althea Gibson became the 1st black competitor in a US national tennis competition.

7th AUG– Tour de France: Ferdinand Kübler became the first Swiss to win the Tour.

26th Aug– Australia beat US (4-1) at the 39th Davis Cup in New York.

29th Aug– The International Olympic Committee voted to admit West Germany and Japan for the next Olympic Games to be held in 1952. Both teams had been banned following WWII.

17th Sep– San Francisco 49ers played their 1st NFL game, losing 21-17.

1st Oct– Babe Zaharias tied Open scoring record (291, par-9) to beat Betsy Rawls by 9 strokes at the US Open Women's Golf, Rolling Hills CC.

31st Oct– The Big Cat, Earl Lloyd became the first African-American to play an NBA game, scoring 6 points for the Washington Capitols.

2nd Dec– South African world bantam weight boxing champion Vic Toweel set a record for knockdowns in a title fight against Englishman Danny Sullivan in Johannesburg. Sullivan floored 14 times in 10 rounds before fighting stopped.

Saves time saves money

Wash and set your hair–then simply relax in your favourite chair–at home. Own a Magicair–and your "appointment only" worries are over. *You* fix the time–*you* name the day–there's no waiting with your own Magicair Hair Dryer.

Magicair is a really professional hair dryer for your home, with a choice of hot or cold drying air. It's well within your budget too.

See how simply the Magicair can be fitted to a table or chair back. No more aching arms–just sit back and read your favourite magazine and the Magicair does the work.

Fashion Trends of the 1950s

With the misery and bleakness of the war years behind us, the 50s were a time to show off. Consumerism was now a way of life and we were all too willing to spend money on luxuries, non-essentials, and fashion.

How we looked and how we dressed became important everyday considerations for women and men. We spent money like never before, guided by our favorite fashion icons, and helped along by a maturing advertising industry which flooded us with fashion advice through newspapers, magazines, billboards, radio and television.

Clothing manufacturers had perfected mass production techniques while providing military uniforms during the war years. They now shifted their focus to well made, stylish, ready-to-wear clothes.

Mothers and babies

Fashions: here and now

Fashions: coming soon

Fall fabrics

Midsummer fiction

Mademoiselle magazine cover, June 1950.

Beauty on Parade A SERIES OF PAINTINGS by DAVID WRIGHT

The American Weekly cover, April 1950.

The American Magazine cover, April 1950.

No longer just for the wealthy, the growing middle classes could now afford to be fashionable. Magazines and mail-order catalogs kept us informed of the latest trends in fashion, make-up, and accessories.

DESCRIPTIONS ON PAGE 42

NEWS MAKERS
by *Susan Lynn*

YOUR CHOICE
OF PAGE $5.99 EACH

Angora Trim
•
Misses' and
Half Sizes

[15]

Capelet Sheath
•
Misses' Sizes
Only

[16]

[14]
2-pc. Crepe
Blouson Dress
•
Misses' and
Junior Sizes

Paris Inspired
Accessories
Hat p. 75
Bag p. 68

[17]
Flannel Sheath
Coat Dress
•
Misses' and
Half Sizes

[18]
Foille Princess
•
Misses' and
Junior Sizes

46 | NATIONAL BELLAS HESS

Dresses from the *National Bellas Hess* mail order catalog in a mix of
the "tea skirt" and "sheath" styles that were popular in the year 1950.

Cashmere Bouquet Lipstick. 8 fashionable shades that go on, stay on, without smearing.

Smoothly, evenly does it with exciting Cashmere Bouquet Lipstick—never a fear of a rub or smear! So clinging, creamy, caressing, your lips take on a *new* look... an *alive* look... one that says, plain as day, "I *dare* you"! And of course no other lipstick, at any price, betters Cashmere Bouquet's range of fashionable reds. Get Cashmere Bouquet today, and then, *try* to go back to your previous brand. Yes, you're sentenced for life... but you'll love it!

In smart new swivel case. Only 25¢
Look your loveliest with Cashmere Bouquet

Christian Dior's "New Look" from 1947.

As with before the war, all eyes looked to Paris for new directions in haute couture. In 1947 Christian Dior didn't disappoint, unveiling his glamorous, extravagant, ultra-feminine "New Look" to the world.

Gone were the boxy tailored jackets with padded shoulders and short skirts. Paris had brought back femininity, with clinched waists, fuller busts and hips, and longer, wider skirts. The emphasis was on abundance. This New Look carried us for more than a decade, well into the 1950s.

The "New Look" in 1950.

To achieve this impossible hour-glass figure, corsets and girdles were sold in record numbers. Metal underwire bras made a comeback, and a new form of bra known as the "cathedral bra" or "bullet bra" became popular.

the very **least** we can do!

ve love to do wonderful
e things to make you feel small
I light and free as the air...little
gs like this, for example...a few inches

Bullet bra and girdle from Jantzen.

Catalog dresses from Spiegel's 1955 Spring-Summer Collection.

Nylons...Sweet 'n Fresh

Free-of-care nylon in fashions that stay crisp
on hottest days, keep you cool 'n fresh always

Despite criticisms against the extravagance of the New Look, and arguments that heavy corsets and paddings undermined the freedoms women had won during the war years, the New Look was embraced on both sides of the Atlantic. Before long, inexpensive, ready-to-wear versions of Dior's New Look had found their way into our department store catalogs.

Dior also created a slimmed down alternative look, with elegant straight skirt and short jacket. This groomed and tailored look, known as the sheath dress, continued to place emphasis on the hourglass figure.

Also known as the "wiggle dress", this sexier figure-hugging silhouette was preferred by movie stars such as Marilyn Monroe.

Women embraced the femininity of 1950s' fashion from head to toe. Hats, scarves, belts, gloves, shoes, stockings, handbags and jewelry were all given due consideration.

Out on the street, no outfit would be complete without a full complement of matching accessories.

"I lived in Milwaukee, I ought to know... Blatz is Milwaukee's finest beer!"

Says Uta Hagen famous star of "Streetcar Named Desire" and many other Broadway hits.

"Wisconsinites like me are used to fine beers," says Uta Hagen. "Because Milwaukee is America's premium beer capital, we always have our choice of the best. And, like most Milwaukeeans, I choose Blatz. It's Milwaukee's *finest* beer!" Yes, *official figures* show that Blatz is the *largest-selling beer in Milwaukee and in all Wisconsin,* too! Try Blatz Beer today!

Uta Hagen's career includes teaching theatre classes, directing experimental productions, playing the piano. She also loves to cook. "My refrigerator is always crowded with good things to eat—and plenty of Blatz Beer, too!" says Uta.

Take a tip from Uta Hagen. Ask for Blatz Beer at your favorite club, tavern, restaurant, or neighborhood store. Remember Blatz is Milwaukee's *finest* beer!

Other News from 1950

31st Jan– Harry S. Truman, President of the USA, ordered the development of a hydrogen (fusion) bomb in direct response to the Soviet detonation of an atomic bomb just four months earlier. Two years later, the US succeeded in creating the more powerful hydrogen bomb, testing it for the first time in the Pacific in 1952. The Soviets tested their first hydrogen bomb in 1953.

8th Feb– The Stasi (Ministry for State Security) was founded in East Germany. Modeled after the Soviet KGB, the Stasi was responsible for both domestic political surveillance and foreign espionage.

12th Feb– Albert Einstein warned of mutual destruction should nuclear war be the eventual outcome of the Cold War.

14th Feb– A mutual defense and assistance treaty was signed by the two communist powers–the Soviet Union and the People's Republic of China– giving the West further argument that communism was a dangerous international movement.

9th May– L. Ron Hubbard published *Dianetics: A Modern Science of Mental Health*. In this book he introduced the self-help concept of Dianetics, which forms the basis of Scientology.

17th Jun– Dr. Richard Lawler performed the world's first successful kidney transplant on patient Ruth Tucker (49) in Illinois USA. The kidney would function for just 53 days, before being removed due to medical complications . Ruth lived a further 5 years.

16th Sep– The Journal of the American Medical Association published two articles outlining a six hundred and eighty-four case study proving the link between cigarette smoking and cancer.

13th Nov– The President of Venezuela, Colonel Carlos Delgado Chalbaud, was kidnapped and murdered in Caracas.

22nd Nov– Shirley Temple announced her retirement from show business at age 22.

13th Dec– James Dean secured his first acting break, playing the part of a fun-loving teenager in a Pepsi Commercial. His good looks and acting talent caught the eye of scouts, who wasted no time launching him to movie star status.

How to take the Labor out
of the Labor Day Week End

Famous People Born in 1950

5th Jan– Chris Stein, American guitarist & co-founder of Blondie.

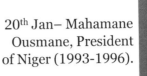

20th Jan– Mahamane Ousmane, President of Niger (1993-1996).

13th Feb– Peter Gabriel, English singer.

18th Feb– Cybill Shepherd, actress.

24th Feb– George Thorogood, American singer & guitarist.

26th Feb– Helen Clark, New Zealand Prime Minister (1999-2008).

27th Feb– Franco Moschino, Italian fashion designer.

2nd Mar– Karen Carpenter, American vocalist & drummer.

4th Mar– Rick Perry, American politician, Governor of Texas (2000-2015).

13th Mar– Bernard Julien, West Indies cricketer.

17th Mar– Betty Dukes, American Walmart employee & discrimination activist.

26th Mar– Alan Silvestri, American film score composer.

30th Mar– Robbie Coltrane, Scottish actor.

5th Apr– Agnetha Fältskog [Anna Ulvaeus], Swedish singer (ABBA).

12th Apr– David Cassidy, American singer & actor.

18th Apr– Kenny Ortega, American film & TV producer.

28th Apr– Jay Leno, American comedian & TV talk show host.

13th May– Stevie Wonder, American singer-songwriter.

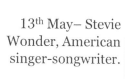

22nd May– Bernie Taupin, British singer & lyricist.

23rd May– Martin McGuinness, Irish Sinn Féin politician & IRA member.

14th Jun– Rowan Williams, 104th Archbishop of Canterbury, UK.

5th July– Huey Lewis, American musician.

15th July– Arianna Huffington, creator of The Huffington Post.

18th July– Richard Branson, British entrepreneur.

9th Aug– Chris Haney, Canadian journalist & creator of "Trivial Pursuit".

11th Aug– Steve Wozniak, co-founder of Apple Computer.

15th Aug– Anne Elizabeth Alice Louise Windsor, British Princess.

1st Sep– Phil McGraw, American psychologist (Dr. Phil).

12th Sep– Gustav Brunner, Austrian Formula One designer & engineer.

7th Sep– Narendra Modi, 15th Prime Minister of India.

21st Sep– Bill Murray, American actor & comedian.

31st Oct– Zaha Hadid, British architect.

1950 in Numbers

Census Statistics [1]

- Population of the world   2.5 billion
- Population in the United States   158.8 million
- Population in the United Kingdom   50.62 million
- Population in Canada   13.73 million
- Population in Australia   8.18 million
- Average age for marriage of women   20.3 years old
- Average age for marriage of men   22.8 years old
- USA divorce rate   26 %
- Average family income USA $3,300 per year
- Minimum wage USA $0.75 per hour

Costs of Goods [2]

- Average home $7,500-$8,500
- Average new car $1,150
- New Cadillac Series 62 $3,650
- A gallon of gas $0.18
- A pack of cigarettes $0.15
- A loaf of bread $0.12
- A gallon of milk $0.82
- T bone steak $0.59 per pound
- Lamb chops $0.49 per pound
- Sliced bacon $0.35 per pound
- Potatoes $0.35 for 5 pounds
- Large eggs $0.49 per dozen
- Kraft cheese slices $0.29 per pack.
- Frozen green beans $0.24 per half pound

[1] Figures taken from worldometers.info/world-population, US National Center for Health Statistics, *Divorce and Divorce Rates* US (cdc.gov/nchs/data/series/sr_21/sr21_029.pdf) and United States Census Bureau, *Historical Marital Status Tables* (census.gov/data/tables/time-series/demo/families/marital.html).
[2] Figures taken from thepeoplehistory.com/1950.html.

Image Attributions

Photographs and images used in this book are reproduced courtesy of the following:

Page 4 – From *Life* Magazine March 27, 1950. Source: books.google.com.sg/books?id=BFMEAAAAMBAJ&printsec. Pre 1978, no copyright mark (Public Domain* (PD) image).

Page 6 – From *LOOK* Magazine Photograph Collection. Source: Library of Congress, Prints & Photographs Division, [Reproduction number e.g., LC-L9-60-8812, frame 8]. Pre 1978, no copyright mark (PD* image).

Page 7 – From the Benjamin Moore House Paint 1950s advertisement. Pre 1978, no copyright mark (PD image).

Page 8 – Westinghouse advertisement source: eBay.com. Pre 1978 no copyright mark (PD image). – Magazine by Science Service Inc. Source: comicbookplus.com/?cbplus=atomic. Pre 1978, no copyright mark (PD image).

Page 9 – Advertisement source: eBay.com. Pre 1978, no copyright mark (PD image).

Page 10 – Victoria Embankment j/w Westminster Bridge by Leonard Bentley. Source: search.creativecommons.org/photos/3d631476-f436-4609-86b4-875edda5c618. License CC BY-SA 2.0 (PD image).

Page 11 – Creator unknown. Pre 1978, no copyright mark (PD image).

Page 12 – From *Life* Magazine, April 24, 1950. Source: books.google.com.sg/books?id=oUkEAAAAMBAJ&printsec. Pre 1978, no copyright mark (PD* image).

Page 13 – Photo source: digital.library.temple.edu/digital/collection/p15037coll3/id/61595. US government owned image. Photographer unknown, (PD image).

Page 14 & 15 – Advertisement source: eBay.com. Pre 1978, no copyright mark (PD image).

Page 16 – Advertisement source: flickr.com/photos/tom-margie/1441181992. Attribution 2.0 Generic (CC BY 2.0).

Page 17 – From *Life* Magazine October 16, 1950. Source: books.google.com.sg/books?id=CEwEAAAAMBAJ&printsec. Pre 1978, no copyright mark (PD* image).

Page 18 – Studio promotional photo of Ed Sullivan. Source: the United States Library of Congress's Prints and Photographs division under the digital ID cph.3c23391. (PD image).

–*The Lone Ranger* promotional photo from ABC Television April 11, 1960. Pre 1978, no copyright mark (PD image).

Page 19 – Promotional poster for *The Bob Hope Show*. Source: loc.gov/exhibits/bobhope/tv. Pre 1978, no copyright mark (PD image). – Ralph Byrd photo source: historiasdecinema.com/2010/09/lembrando-grandes-seriados-2. Pre 1978, no copyright mark (PD image). – George Fenneman and Groucho Marx from the radio version of *You Bet Your Life* by NBC Radio. Source: commons.wikimedia.org/wiki/File:George_Fenneman_and_Groucho_Marx_You_Bet_Your_Life_1951.jpg (PD image). – Jack Benny photo from MCA. Source: commons.wikimedia.org/wiki/File:Jack_Benny_and_vault.JPG. Pre 1978, no copyright mark (PD image).

Page 20 – Photo by Roger Higgins,1965 World Telegram staff photographer, donated to the United States Library of Congress's Prints and Photographs division the digital ID cph.3f06148. Source: commons.wikimedia.org/wiki/File:Charles_Schulz_NYWTS.jpg (PD image).

Pages 20 & 21 – Reproductions of *Charlie Brown and Gang*. Reproductions are included here for information only under U.S. fair use laws due to: 1- No free alternative can exist of trademarked characters; 2- images are low resolution copies; 3- this does not limit the copyright owner's rights to sell the comic strip in any way; 4- Copies are too small to be used to make illegal copies for another book; 5- The images are significant to the article created.

Page 22 – Advertisement source: flickr.com/photos/tom-margie/1415323095/. Attribution-ShareAlike 2.0 Generic (CC BY-SA 2.0).

Page 23 – Advertisement source: restaurant-ingthroughhistory.com. Pre 1978, no copyright mark (PD image). – Diners Card photo. Photographer unknown. Source: economic-definition.com/Financial/Kreditnaya_karta_Credit_card__eto.html. Creator unknown. Pre 1978, no copyright mark (PD image).

Page 24 – Advertisement source: loc.gov/pictures/item/2004668529/ (PD image).

Page 26 – US tank and crew, source: commons.wikimedia.org/wiki/File:HA-SC-98-06983-Crew_of_M24_along_Naktong_River_front-Korean_war-17_Aug_1950.JPEG. Camera Operator: SGT. RILEY. US Federal Government owned (PD image). Camera Operator: SGT. RILEY. US Federal Government owned (PD image). – US soldiers photo source: commons.wikimedia.org/wiki/File:KoreanWarFallenSoldier1.jpg. Image by U.S. Army, US Federal Government owned (PD image). – Chinese tanks photo. Source: forum.worldoftanks.ru. Photographer unknown, Pre 1978, no copyright mark (PD image).

Page 27 – Allied army in Korea photos source: commons.wikimedia.org/wiki/Category:United_States_Army_in_the_Korean_War. Crown copyright work owned by the Australian Government. Photographer unknown, (PD image). – Canadian army, source: i.dailymail.co.uk/i/newpix/2018/05/31/20/4CCA9CBB00000578-5789731-image-a-20_1527795199977.jpg. – British army in Korea photos source: home.bt.com/news/on-this-day/june-25-1950-invasion-from-communist-north-sparks-the-start-of-the-korean-war-11363988570216. Crown copyright work owned by the British Government. Photographer unknown, (PD image).

Page 28 – All movie posters source: rottentomatoes.com. Reproductions are included here for information only under U.S. fair use laws due to: 1- No free alternative can exist of antique posters; 2- images are low resolution copies; 3- these do not limit the copyright owners' rights to sell the posters in any way; 4- Copies are too small to be used to make illegal copies for another book; 5- The images are significant to the article created.

Page 29 – Soviet poster, 1950. Source: votefraud.org/josef_stalin_vote_fraud_page.htm. – Bulgarian poster, 1950. Source: foreignmovieposters.tumblr.com/post/145135462086/liberated-china-1950-bulgarian-poster. – Sino-Soviet posters, 1950. Source: cccpism.com/book/zhongsu/pic.htm. All posters pre 1978, no copyright mark (PD image).

Page 30 – Photos: sahistory.org.za/article/group-areas-act-1950, and religiouseftlaw.com/2014/04/index.html photographers unknown. Pre 1978, no copyright mark (PD image).

Page 31 – Danger sign, from a farm sign in Johannesburg. 1st July 1952. Source: commons.wikimedia.org/wiki/Category:Apartheid_signage Pre 1978, no copyright mark (PD image). – Caution sign, source: fr.igihe.com/IMG/arton16496.jpg?1451940393, photographer unknown. Pre 1978, no copyright mark (PD image).

Page 32 – TWA poster, 1950. Source: commons.wikimedia.org/wiki/File:TWA_Italy_Poster_(18857334053).jpg (PD image). – Northwest Airlines poster, 1950. Source: vintageadbrowser.com/airlines-and-aircraft-ads-1950s/7. – Air France poster, 1950. Source: flickr.com/photos/estampemoderne/5842503124. Attribution-NoDerivs 2.0 Generic (CC BY-ND 2.0). – Air Liban poster, 1950. Source: en.artprecium.com/images/photos/21/5c8273b4dc6bf.jpg. Pre 1978, no copyright mark (PD image).

Page 33 – Indian Stamp, 1950. Source: commons.wikimedia.org/wiki/File:1950_Republic_India_04.jpg (PD image). – Street procession: merepix.com/2013/01/india-first-republic-day-celebrations-jan-26-1950-photos.html photographer unknown. Pre 1978, no copyright mark (PD image).

Page 34 – Advertisement source: ebay.ie. Pre 1978, no copyright mark (PD image).

Page 35 – 1950 Trade advertisement for an Australian documentary. Source: tutorversal.com/blog/xxi-commonwealth-games-2018-the-story-so-far.html. Pre 1978, no copyright mark (PD image).

Page 36 – From *Life* Magazine, Oct 16, 1950. Source: books.google.com.sg/books?id=CEwEAAAAMBAJ&printsec. Pre 1978, no copyright mark (PD* image).

Page 37 – Joseph McGinnis, 1956. Source: fbi.gov/history/famous-cases/brinks-robbery. Pre 1978, no copyright mark (PD image). – Mug shots of the Brinks robbers, 1956. Source: robertallisonhistory.wordpress.com/2020/04/16/the-brinks-robber-crime-of-the-century/. Pre 1978, no copyright mark (PD image).

Page 38 – Still image from the film *The Men*, 1950. Source: imdb.com. This is a low-resolution image for information only, reproduced under fair use terms. It is believed that this image will not devalue the ability of the copyright holder to profit from the original work. – 1951 film poster. Source: en.wikipedia.org/wiki/A_Streetcar_Named_ Desire_(1951_film). (PD image).
Page 39 – Still image from the film *The Wild One*, 1953. Source: kinopoisk.ru/picture/1947898/ (PD image). – Still image from the film *Marc Anthony*, 1950. Source: flickr.com/photos/jumborois/3354472656/ (PD image). – Still image from the film *The Godfather*, 1972. Source: en.wikipedia.org/wiki/Vito_Corleone. This is a low-resolution image for information only, reproduced under fair use terms. It is believed that this image will not devalue the ability of the copyright holder to profit from the original work. – Still image from the film *On the Waterfront*, 1954. Source: flickr.com/photos/classicvintage/9316236341. Attribution Attribution 4.0 International (CC BY 4.0).
Page 40 – Still image from the film *Fancy Pants*. Source: imdb.com. This is a low-resolution image for information only, reproduced under fair use terms. It is believed that this image will not devalue the ability of the copyright holder to profit from the original work. – *Rio Grande* publicity still. Source: commons.wikimedia.org/wiki/Category: Rio_Grande_(film). Permission PD-US no copyright notice. (PD image). – Publicity photo of Marilyn Monroe. Source: commons.wikimedia.org/wiki/File:Monroe_1953_publicity.jpg (PD image).
Page 41 – 1950 *Cinderella* film poster. Source: commons.wikimedia.org/wiki/Category:Cinderella_(1950_film). (PD image). – 1950 *Father of the Bride* poster. Source: wikivisually.com/wiki/File:FatheroftheBride1950.jpg. This is a low-resolution image for information only, reproduced under fair use terms. It is believed that this image will not devalue the ability of the copyright holder to profit from the original work. – *King Solomon's Mines* 1950 film poster. Source: flickr.com/photos/jumborois/2816930851/. (PD image).
Page 42 – Theatrical poster from 1950. Source: upload.wikimedia.org/wikipedia/commons/c/cc/Guys-and-Dolls-Original-Poster.jpg. Attribution-ShareAlike 4.0 International (CC BY-SA 4.0). – Promotional stage photo. Source: fanpix.famousfix.com/gallery/robert-alda/p101956377. Pre 1978, no copyright mark (PD image). – Cinema poster from 1955. Source: famousfix.com/topic/guys-and-dolls. Pre 1978, no copyright renewal (PD image).
Page 43 – Book cover and film posters. Source: en.wikipedia.org/wiki/The_Lion,_the_Witch_and_the_Wardrobe. These are low-resolution images for information only, reproduced under fair use terms. It is believed that these images will not devalue the ability of the copyright holders to profit from the original works.
Page 44 – Guy Lombardo in 1944. Source: wikivisually.com/wiki/Guy_Lombardo from Music Corporation of America-photo by Maurice Seymour, Chicago. Permission PD-PRE1978 (PD image). – Nat King Cole in 1952, source: commons.wikimedia.org/wiki/Category:Nat_King_Cole by GAC-General Artists Corporation (management). Permission PD-PRE1978 (PD image). –Sammy Kaye source: wikivisually.com/wiki/Sammy_Kaye by MCA-Music Corporation of America; photographer: James Kriegsmann, New York Permission PD-PRE1978 (PD image). –Patti Page source: wikivisually.com/wiki/Patti_Page by General Artists Corporation (management). Permission PD-PRE1978 (PD image).
Page 45 – Perry Como by NBC Television, 1956. Source: commons.wikimedia.org/wiki/File:Perry_Como_1956.JPG. Permission PD-PRE1978 (PD image). – Bing Crosby. Source: commons.wikimedia.org/wiki/File:Bing_Crosby,_1942. jpg. Creative Commons CC0 1.0 Universal Public Domain Dedication.
Page 46 – From *Life* Magazine March 24, 1950. Source: books.google.com.sg/books?id=BFMEAAAAMBAJ&printsec. Pre 1978, no copyright mark (PD* image).
Page 47 – Photograph by BRDC/Silverstone Experience. Source: welt.de/sport/formel1/plus207948105/70-Jahre-Formel-1-Waehrend-meiner-Karriere-starben-65-Fahrer.html. – 1950 Poster. Source: progcovers.com/motor/ montecarlo.html. Permission PD-PRE1978 (PD image). – Guiseppe Farina. Source: dummysports.com/1950-f1/. Photographer unknown. Pre 1978, no copyright mark (PD image).
Page 48 – Advertisement by Liggett & Myers Tobacco Company, 1950. Source: Stanford Research into the Impact of Tobacco Advertising, (PD image).
Page 49 – Demaret, source: golfhistorytoday.com/jimmy-demaret-born-1910/. Pre 1978, no copyright mark (PD image). – Cooper, source: basketball.fandom.com/wiki/Chuck_Cooper. Pre 1978, no copyright mark (PD image).
Page 50 – Kübler, source: capovelo.com/oldest-living-tour-de-france-winner-ferdinand-ferdi-kubler-dies/. Creator unknown. Pre 1978, no copyright mark (PD image). – Toweel, source: alchetron.com/Vic-Toweel. Creator unknown. Pre 1978, no copyright mark (PD image).
Page 51 – Advertisement source: flickr.com/photos/vintageimagenook/28713746517/. Public Domain Mark 1.0
Page 54 – Advertisement source: imgur.com/gallery/F6UwKM2. Pre 1978, no copyright mark (PD image).
Page 55 – Advertisement source: flickr.com/photos/nesster/5514151747/. Attribution 4.0 International (CC BY 4.0).
Page 56 – Photo by Lars Nordin, CC BY 4.0, Source: commons.wikimedia.org/w/index.php?curid=39208366. Licensed under Creative Commons Attribution 4.0 International.
Page 57 – Jantzen advert. Source: flickr.com/photos/nesster/5521936717/. Attribution 4.0 International (CC BY 4.0)
Page 58 – Marilyn Monroe in 1952 studio publicity portrait for film Niagara, by 20th Century Fox. (PD image). – Models walking photo. Source: Jessica at myvintagevogue.com. Licensed under CC BY 2.0.
Page 59 – From *Life* April 24, 1950. Source: books.google.com.sg/books?id=oUkEAAAAMBAJ&printsec. Pre 1978, no copyright mark (PD* image).
Page 60 – Harry Truman, Source: Library of Congress's Prints and Photographs division under the digital ID cph 3c17122 (PD image). – Albert Einstein, Source: Library of Congress's Prints and Photographs division under the digital ID cph.3b46036 (PD image).
Page 61 – Smoking women, creator unknown. Pre 1978, no copyright mark (PD image). – Shirley Temple, source: uk.wikipedia.org/wiki/Ширлі_Темпл. Pre 1978, no copyright mark (PD image). – James Dean Studio promotional photo, source: af.wikipedia.org/wiki/James_Dean#/media/Lêer:James_Dean_ca_1955.jpg. Pre 1978, no copyright mark (PD image).
Page 62 – Advertisement source: imgur.com/gallery/GQ8T4. Pre 1978, no copyright mark (PD image).
Page 63 – Advertisement source: flickr.com/photos/dok1/8583523120/. Attribution 4.0 International (CC BY 4.0).
Page 64 & 65 – All photos are, where possible, CC BY 2.0 or PD images made available by the creator for free use including commercial use. Where commercial use photos are unavailable, photos are included here for information only under U.S. fair use laws due to: 1- images are low resolution copies; 2- images do not devalue the ability of the copyright holders to profit from the original works in any way; 3- Images are too small to be used to make illegal copies for use in another book; 4- The images are relevant to the article created.
Page 66 – From *Life* Magazine March 27, 1950. Source: books.google.com.sg/books?id=BFMEAAAAMBAJ&printsec. Pre 1978, no copyright mark (PD* image).

These words first appeared in print in the year 1950.

BRAINWASHING

hot potato

broad-spectrum

deep fryer

multimedia

off-the-shelf

epoxy resin

Private Label

Cardiac arrest

Ballistic Missile

bioengineering

SPIN OFF

Space shuttle

shopping mall

MUG SHOT

ACTION FIGURE

nail-biter

* From merriam-webster.com/time-traveler/1950.

Please help me out:

I sincerely hope you enjoyed reading this book and that it brought back many fond memories from the past.

I have enjoyed researching and writing this book for you and would greatly appreciate your feedback by way of a written review and/or star rating.

First and foremost, I am always looking to grow and improve as a writer. It is reassuring to hear what works, as well as to receive constructive feedback on what could improve.

Second, starting out as an unknown author is exceedingly difficult, and Customer Reviews go a long way toward making the journey out of anonymity possible.

Please help me by taking a few moments to leave a review for others to read.

Best regards,
Bernard Bradforsand-Tyler.

Please leave a
book review/rating at:

http://bit.ly/1950reviews

Or scan the QR code:

Made in the USA
Middletown, DE
14 November 2021